To Anita + Steve
Love L

The Tin Lady

Tens of Tips for Charity Tin Collecting

by

Leonie Lewis

Published in 2021 by

Russell House Publishing Ltd
The Coach House
Ware
Lyme Regis
Dorset
DT7 3RH

Tel: 01297 443948
e-mail: jan@russellhouse.co.uk
www.russellhouse.co.uk

British Library Cataloguing-in-Publication Data:
A catalogue record for this book is available from the British Library.

ISBN: 978-1-9160276-5-7

Typeset by: Kerry Press Ltd, St Albans, Hertfordshire

Printed by: CPI, Antony Rowe, Wiltshire

Contents

Contents

Acknowledgements

This guide would not have happened without the active involvement of some wonderful people.

Taryn, my creative graphic designer and friend who took the written words and created illustrations just for this guide, as a favour to me.

My cousin Julia who not only made incisive comments, but painstakingly read each chapter and corrected my careless grammar!

Kathy, a new friend from across the pond, who suggested the brilliant title.

Ken, who told me not to give up, and Jan the publisher who had enough belief in me and liked the idea of this book enough to publish it.

I also want to acknowledge my hubby, Howard who told me what I shouldn't write!

About the Author

Leonie is married to Howard, and lives in the leafy suburb of pinner, Greater London.

She is a member of the Pinner United Synagogue Community and has worked as both a professional and volunteer in the charity and voluntary sector for over forty years.

She has a Masters in the Sociology of Education, an MBA (Master of Business Administration) in Educational Leadership, and was awarded an MBE in 2018, not forgetting her BGA (Best Grandma Award)!

About the Illustrator

Taryn Honickberg is a graphic designer with over seventeen years' experience.

She specialises in producing creative designs and marketing materials for the charity, volunteer and commercial sectors.

Taryn can be contacted by e-mailing taryn@ctbcreative.com.

Foreword

Charity fundraising is in a time of crisis and change. The Covid-19 virus restrictions to our way of life have closed down or dramatically reduced many ways of giving, while paradoxically creating new ones - encouraging many more people to give some of their time to help tackle the crisis in all kinds of ways. Organising these new recruits, in tandem with the more long-standing army of volunteers, in the face of rapidly dwindling financial resources is one of the biggest challenges the UK voluntary sector has ever seen.

Creating possible routes to a new fundraising future requires an understanding of the complex jigsaw of methods that have served us so well in the past – some of which may well return in different forms as the Covid-19 crisis subsides. In this book Leonie Lewis gives commendable priority to one aspect of fundraising that has served the sector well over the years – the casual street collections delivered by rattlers of tins or enabled by charity boxes installed on counters in small shops and pubs. She takes us back to biblical times where the idea first surfaced - for the upkeep of the temple; to the charity collectors that swarmed through the streets to raise money for the survivors of the Great Fire of London; and how a philanthropist organised the world's earliest formal street collection for widows and children of lifeboat volunteers.

But this book goes beyond history to record the approaches and motivation of the army of volunteers who shake the boxes and tins, as well as the attitudes and reactions of members of the public who dip into their pockets to respond – and those who do not!

It also acknowledges that change is on the way, as we move inexorably towards a cashless society. Has that been hastened by the long months of Covid-19 when cash has almost become taboo? Or will the small change in the pocket return to give a new lease of life for street collectors when life returns to normal. Some of the bigger charities are not taking any chances on that front – and are examining an increasing number of innovative ways to use contactless cards in their fundraising.

So, the jury is out on whether the familiar street collections outside Tesco or Sainsburys will return to the same extent – or in the same way - as before. But whatever the shape of spontaneous methods of charity fundraising in the future, their creators will want to draw on the rich experiences of this journey through a normally under-reported type of fundraising that has served the voluntary sector so well over the years. Driven by a passionate charity street collector, this book is both a valuable guide and a recruiting sergeant for those who would follow in her footsteps.

Sir Martyn Lewis CBE
Broadcaster, Volunteer and former Chairman of the National Council for Voluntary Services (2010-16).

Chapter 1: Introduction

For close to ten years, I have been volunteering as a charity tin collector. Not collecting charity boxes, but fundraising for my local Mencap, Harrow Mencap.

Mencap is the leading voice of learning disability in the UK, 'everything we **do** is about valuing and supporting people with a learning disability, and their families and carers. Our vision is a world where people with a learning disability are valued equally, listened to and included'.

Harrow Mencap is an independent charity and a multi-project service provider supporting people with learning disabilities and their families. We are proud of our local reputation as the primary campaigning organisation for people with learning disabilities in Harrow.

Over the years, I have had some interesting experiences as a charity tin collector; some funny, some sad, and others, just-plain weird and wacky. I felt compelled to put pen to paper, not just for me, but also for anyone who collects for charity at a supermarket holding [rattling] a collection box.

This guide is not quite a manual for charity tin collecting, although it shares some pertinent observations. It is perhaps more of an examination about us volunteer collectors and those members of the general public who drop money into our collecting boxes, as well as those who choose not to.

This review is not confined to the physical action of placing money into a tin, or contributing to charity in this way, but examines how this showcases us as human beings, some kind and generous, others less so, and many of us often sadly indifferent.

Whilst there are myriads of charities in the UK, all deserving of funds and donations (some, more deserving than others), if everyone were to give just ten pence a week to charity, the charitable sector in the UK would be far stronger and more sustainable.

According to the latest NCVO 2019 Almanac, of the sector's total £45.5bn income, £10.1bn comes from donations by individuals. The Charities Aid Foundation's annual UK Giving report, suggests the average donation amount at around £40. It also found that cash is the most common way of giving in all age groups, with 58 per cent saying they had donated this way.

'We rightly celebrate the enduring generosity of the UK, and we do rank among the most generous in the world. But that spirit of giving is not something that our charities, our politicians and our wider communities can ever take for granted...

This year's CAF UK Giving survey shows that yet again the key measuresof giving are on a downward path. For the third year running significantly fewer people say they are giving money. The overall estimate of household giving in the UK is relatively stable in cash terms at £10.1bn, but that is a result of a smaller group of dedicated donors giving more'.

Sir John Low Former Chief Executive of the Charities Aid Foundation 2019. Caf-uk-giving-2019-report, May 2019, Foreword, page 3.

Neil Heslop, the current Chief Executive of the Charities Aid Foundation, noted that CAF research has found the UK to be one of the most generous countries in the world. This shows not only the huge generosity of the UK public, but great faith in the work of our much-loved charities. Fundraisers and fundraising play an integral role in enabling this vital work to continue.

January 2021.

Chapter 2: About Turn

About Me

As a member of the Jewish faith, I am mindful of the religious obligation to give away 10% of my earnings, and I do try to live by this principle. As I write during the first UK Covid-19 lockdown and continued pandemic, the numerous demands on my 10% donation are multiplied, so I apologise to those charities to which I had previously donated, as others have assumed a more immediate priority. Indeed, a separate chapter is dedicated to fundraising for charities during this pandemic. (I have written as a postscript about collecting at this time, please refer to chapter 9).

Being over 60, and retired from full-time work in the charity sector, I am now a charity and community consultant, and yes, I do have a lot to say about the sector, but that is for another book.

I happened to notice a gap in the book market about raising money via collection tins and buckets and decided to focus on this neglected area.

Since the UK charity market relies so heavily on the volunteer tin collection and this type of fundraising, it seemed a topic worthy of **recounting** – get it, counting!

In The Collection Tin, an article by Sam Butler in SOFII (Showcase of Funding Innovation and Inspiration, 2016), it was noted that an average tin will generate £260 per annum. There are 17,500 registered newsagents in the UK, this equates to £4.5 million pounds per year.

There are also 35,000 independent retailers in the UK and 48,000 pubs. This amounts to a further £12 million per year.

So, just from these static points – each having just one tin – the revenue generated could reach approximately £26 million. A lot of small change really does add up. www.sofii.org The collection Tin, 10th February 2016.

In 2018 CAF, (Charities Aid Foundation), noted that donations of loose change could be worth an estimated £320m a year to the charities.

Civilsociety.co.uk/news/donations-of-loose-change-worth-320m-a-year-for-charity-says-caf-html, (Civil Society News, 15th May 2018).

About this guide

This guide should be considered as an aide for all us collectors. I share some illustrated tips on maximising the collection experience, and profile the various types of people I have encountered, suggesting how to approach them.

The intention of this guide is to help charity tin collectors raise more money for their given charity. If it helps recruit volunteers, that would be a bonus. Most importantly, it might persuade individuals to part with their cash, and drop coins (or better notes) into the tin.

How I came to be a collector?

Firstly, I was asked.....
Secondly, I was asked .....
Thirdly, I was asked!

Asking or inviting someone to get involved with a project or any activity means you have to be persuasive and understand about a 'relational invitation approach'.

To encourage volunteers, you must not only consider what will work best for the project need, but also the notion of inviting people to engage. Here are two suggestions:

- Make them feel guilty, while at the same time, needed
- Always explain the ease of the task and how they could offer so much, as they have so much to offer.

Having spent over thirty years in the voluntary sector both volunteering and recruiting volunteers, these are the tried and tested ways to get anyone to volunteer. It worked on me!!!

Here is my story ....

I was standing outside my local Marks and Spencer food store, when confronted by an earnest, eager, and slightly dishevelled collector, holding a tin. As he pointed this in my direction, he somewhat surprisingly asked me if I would also like to collect for Harrow Mencap. I had been considering putting money into the tin but was rather taken aback by the directness of the question. After all, I was only going into the store to buy some fruit. "Ummm, I replied, let me think about it, I'm just going in to get some shopping, I'll catch you on the way out!"

My quick response was, of course, to buy myself time, intending that when I had finished, I would make a surreptitious beeline for the exit.

Ha! Twenty minutes later, I was spotted again. The same individual approached me and simply said, "Can we talk? I work for Harrow Mencap and we are looking for volunteers to collect outside supermarkets, it is only once a month or so for two to three hours, and all you need to do is stand outside the supermarket to help us raise much needed funds".

That was it, I was hooked! I dropped my £1 coin in his tin, gave my details and was told I would receive my collecting card in the post and information by email very soon.

Simple, eh? I was now a volunteer charity tin collector!! I had been hooked by the persuasive oratory of this key fundraiser.

I later discovered that he was the co-ordinator for all Harrow Mencap fundraising, and that fundraising through charity tin collecting, was his main priority, as well as engaging would be collectors - this was his undoubted forte!

He had explained the value of volunteering for Harrow Mencap, had given me clear instructions and information about what was required as a collector for the charity via supermarkets, the type of venue where I would be collecting, the timings and basic administrative details about the role, including how often I would need to volunteer.

A week later my Harrow Mencap lanyard was received in the post together with some information about the charity. I had also received instructions by email giving me the date and time I would be required to volunteer, where I needed to be, from whom I should collect the tin and to whom I would return it.

I was given a few dos and don'ts, including the requirement to write my name, the date and time of collecting on the base of the tin. And that was it. Later, over coffee in Morrison's in Hatch End, I was informed that I was now officially a Harrow Mencap collector and would be required to sign in and out of stores for security purposes, not forgetting to inform the duty manager of my whereabouts while on supermarket premises.

Chapter 3: History Lesson

With thanks to IWITOT, (I Wish I'd thought of That), The Temple Times, September 2015.

It is thought that the original collection tin was placed outside the first temple in Jerusalem. The high priest was concerned that the temple was in need of renovation, so he put a tin outside the main entrance. This meant that those who were passing or attending prayer could easily make donations to help with the temple's upkeep.

Later, if we travel forward several thousand years, there is mention of collection tins in Samuel Pepys's diary of 1666. He describes walking home whilst being swamped with charity collectors, all shaking their tins to raise money for the victims of the Great Fire of London.

Following the Mexico disaster, (400 ton Hamburg barque, which ran aground on the perilous sandbanks in the Ribble Estuary near Southport), on the 9th December 1886, which resulted in the loss of 27 lifeboatmen, from Lytham, St Anne's and Southport, a small team organised an event in Manchester that changed the face of fundraising forever.

In 1891, a local wealthy industrialist Sir Charles Macara answered the RNLI's call for help, following a lifeboat disaster.

Five years earlier, 27 men from Southport and St Anne's died trying to rescue sailors from the stricken vessel 'Mexico'.
The RNLI asked for funds and Sir Charles responded in style.
He was so concerned for the widows and children of the volunteers lost that he decided to organise a collection for them. Instead of asking wealthy

1891: The world's first street collection for the Royal National Lifeboat Institute in Manchester

philanthropists for money, he appealed to the man on the street. Charles and his wife Marion got a committee together and organised the first Lifeboat Saturday in aid of the appeal.

It was the world's first charity street collection ever recorded, and the formula proved popular for decades to come.

Sir Charles Macara, organiser of the first Lifeboat Saturday

Every tin can that has ever been rattled in high streets up and down the British Isles owes its provenance to this first official tin collection and the sad events that prompted it.

The public turned out in such numbers and responded so generously to that first street collection, it was a sign of the very special respect, regard and affection in which the British people hold their lifeboat men and women, the heroes of the RNLI.

The collection tin is a means to raise unrestricted levels of cash and has been a stalwart of community fund raising for many years. Despite its longevity it is still an effective way to raise money. It manages to keep philanthropy at the forefront of our minds and helps maintain a culture of giving within our community. It reminds people that collectively, we can raise enough to help those who are in need of charity.

A lot of small change really does add up, and although the collecting tin is a rather old-fashioned way to raise funds, it remains a fundamental part of fund raising. Despite technological advances such as crowdfunding and online appeals, cash collection still has a major role to play in supporting charities. And whilst people still have loose or small change in their pockets, the collecting tin is in a league of its own.

Although not so very long ago, people would happily place their loose change into a charity collection box, without much thought to the cause, one of the challenges for collecting today is that the public is pressurised by so many more appeals. Potential donors suffer from so called 'giving fatigue'.

There are exceptions, as we do support calls for major disaster relief, and often respond generously to direct appeals on behalf of a charity, such as Captain Tom Moore's NHS Covid-19 appeal:-

*Captain Tom Moore's extraordinary fundraising efforts

Captain Tom began raising funds for the NHS Charities to thank the magnificent NHS staff who helped him with treatment for cancer and a broken hip. With the aid of a walking frame, he hoped to walk 100 laps of the 25 metre (82 foot) loop of his garden in, Bedfordshire before his 100 Birthday on the 30th April 2020, but in-fact he completed his challenge by the 17th April. Captaintom.org.

On that day, when the amount raised totalled £17 million, JustGiving confirmed it was the largest total ever raised in a single campaign on its site and was the fastest growing campaign on their platform,

Justgiving.com/fundraising/tomswalk.

His donation page closed at midnight on Thursday 1st May 2020, at the end of his birthday, at which point he had raised a total of £32,794,701 from more than, 1.5 million supporters. A message on his page said he was now *'putting his feet up!'*.

* Sadly, Sir Captain Tom Moore passed away in February 2021.

There are continuous and often competing requests for charitable aid. People are now less likely to give as a matter of course. It is getting harder out there on the streets for the volunteers holding their charity tins.

A cashless society

Another challenging development is the now common response: *'sorry I really don't have any change or cash on me'.* We are an increasingly cashless society, and this inevitably impacts on the effectiveness of tin collections.

People are using less cash across the board. As we switch to paying via contactless cards or mobile devices, the result is that most of us are physically carrying smaller amounts of loose change.

A survey at the end of 2016 estimated that an average person carried less than £5 on their person. At around the same time, Pennies, a mobile micropayment donation platform, carried out research which determined that 58 per cent of people had given to charity using a donation tin – and that this was the most popular form of giving. So, there is still a role for charity tin collecting – we just need to adapt to the times.

Civil Society News, Civil Society Media, www.civilsociety.co.uk.

Chapter 4: Local Knowledge

Collecting in my neighbourhood

My local collecting area is Harrow, a large London Borough with a diverse population. Whilst I have collected in several parts of Harrow, the most prevalent one has been my local neighbourhood of Pinner.

Pinner was first recorded as a village in 1231 in the Domesday Book, and still retains its village feel. Well located, and close to the Metropolitan line with good road and rail access to Harrow and Central London, Pinner is just 12 miles northwest of Charing Cross. It is a green leafy district, primarily middle class, which developed because of the underground links.

Like most of Harrow, Pinner has become a more faith diverse area with large communities of Hindus and Muslims, as well as other religious groups including my own, the Jewish Community. We have several synagogues in the borough, a mosque in Harrow, the Zoroastrian centre in Rayners Lane as well as many different churches, all providing for the needs of this multi-faith neighbourhood.

Street wise, in terms of its square footage size, Pinner is relatively small, but extends to include the areas of Pinner Green, Hatch End, Rayners Lane and parts of Eastcote and North Harrow.

While still maintaining its village atmosphere, Pinner is also very well served by all of the major supermarkets, there are five, within a two to three-mile radius, And I have been fortunate to have collected outside all of them except the Lidl, a relatively new addition to the supermarket chains in our location. In fact, I have not seen anybody collect at this store, so it might not be on the charity collectors list YET.

It is important to describe the area, in order, to explain my collecting experiences which occurred when I had positioned myself outside these supermarkets.

Supermarket Charity Tin Rating?

At the back of this guide in Appendix 1, there is a list of my local supermarkets, where I have also collected, as well as those slightly further a-field, including Ruislip, Kingsbury, Edgware, South Harrow and Harrow town centre. Each store is given a trip advisor style tin rating, **not for their food sales but as collecting venues!!!!**

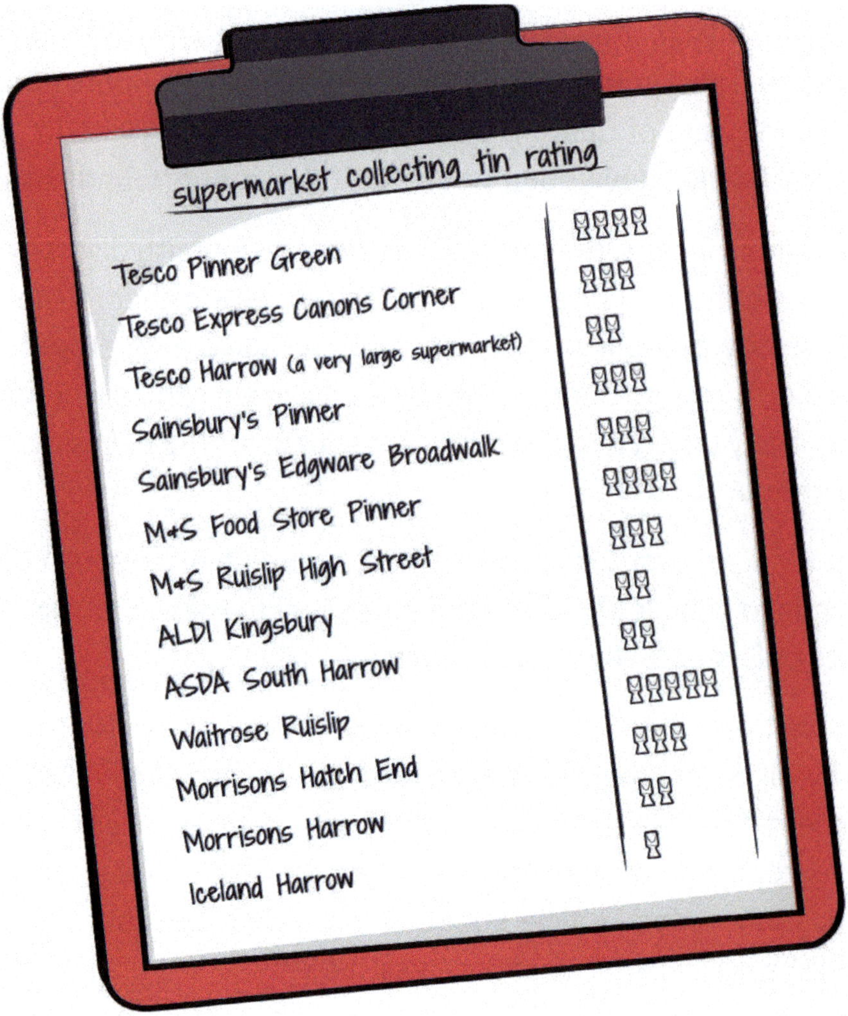

Most of these supermarkets fall within the London Borough of Harrow, whist others touch Brent and Barnet. Harrow Mencap services its clients from these districts too. Memorable collecting experiences at several of these shops are set out in an ensuing chapter.

For the record, as well as fear of being barred from shopping locally, I must point out, I have no particular preferences regarding the food or other goods sold in any of the stores, I know they all do sterling work - my experiences relate purely to collecting for charity.

Supermarkets are given a tin rating in the following areas: -

- Ease of parking, and any associated parking costs
- Space given for collecting
- Friendliness and help offered by staff.

The assessments are based solely on my personal experiences and observations. Whilst not undertaking any formal research or retail analysis, I would reflect that my ratings were probably affected by some, or all of the following:

- Size of the store
- Proximity to other shops
- Location
- Mix of the community
- The time of day, day of the week or indeed, the time of year.

These factors must and do make a difference to the level of giving, and to would be collectors and charities.

Chapter 5: A funny thing happened on the way to.....

During my years in charity tin collection I have had some very interesting experiences, mostly good, and a selection of these I share here.

But I will start with the worst episode. I was collecting one Sunday morning outside Marks and Spencer in Pinner, this is one of my favourite stores and I knew exactly where I had to stand to be seen and to make myself and my presence felt.

Invariably, I make remarks such as, *'Would you like to support Harrow Mencap today? Have you any loose change, Please put a few coppers in the tin, Let me lighten your load, Any loose change in your purse or your pockets?'.* etc, etc, doing my normal stand-up routine with a smile, and always saying *'Good morning'* or *'Good afternoon'.*

That day, a Sunday, I was doing my usual collection tin repartee when I saw walking towards me three, or maybe four elderly women, wearing hats and carrying handbags. It was a scene reminiscent of the Coronation Street I remember watching as a child in the 1960s. These determined looking ladies advanced towards me, exclaiming sharply, *"How dare you collect today on God's day. You shouldn't be standing here. It's an offence and we're going to report you"*. I think this was probably around four years into my charity collecting, and I had never previously been reported to anybody. Understandably, I was a little shaken by their words and concerned by the course of action they threatened to take.

I wasn't convinced that they would contact the manager of the store, but sadly they did. The manager approached me and said rather reluctantly that I could stand outside but I had to remain silent and suggested that Sunday was perhaps not the best day for charity collecting.

I knew, the manager would report this back to the charity, and I was upset that I, a volunteer, had been ticked off for doing something I believed to be worthwhile - supporting a good cause - a charity.

After the senior citizens left the area, the manager came out to me again and told me not to worry. But he did say that the women were very irate and angry that I was collecting on a Sunday. I explained that I had understood that I was not doing anything untoward and that our charity often collected on Sundays, which was a popular shopping day. When I reported this episode back to my manager at the charity, he heard me out and nothing more happened. Indeed, he was upset that I had been distressed about the situation and we continued to collect at this store and on the same days!

That was the first and last time I have ever been reported to anyone. The following Sunday I was at the same supermarket and ready to do battle with the ladies... but they did not show up and I never saw them again.

On a very different note, I recollect another significant experience at the same store, a gentleman approached me, folded a ten-pound note and placed it into my tin. When someone puts a note in your tin you always remember.

On this occasion, a very nice man, similar in age and height to myself, came up to me and told me that he had been a psychiatric nurse, specialising in people with special needs, and had a lot of empathy for the charity Mencap. He then removed a ten-pound note from his wallet and put it in the tin.

A couple of weeks later outside the same store, I saw him again. I have always had a very good memory for faces and as he came towards me, I said, *'Hello, how are you?'*. At which point he took out another ten-pound note for my tin. He then told me the following distressing story.

"When I saw you last time" he said, *"I mentioned that I was a psychiatric nurse, but I didn't mention where I worked, and that I had been a senior psychiatric nurse in Broadmoor".* He went on to say, *"I'm very embarrassed about what happened at the hospital, as I was working in a senior position at the time, and I want you to look out in the press for a story about Jimmy Savile which will be coming out in the next week or two ....it's shocking and disturbing".*

The retired nurse told me that Savile had been given an office at the hospital with key unrestricted access to ward areas, dayrooms and patient rooms. A little uncertain as to what he was referring, I refrained from asking more about the situation, although I was aware at the time, October/ November of 2014, of rumours about Jimmy Savile and sexual abuse at the BBC. He told me how sickened he had felt by what had happened, and I often wonder if, by sharing his horrific story and putting money in my tin, this was his way of apologising. This particular story was upsetting, and this generous donor was clearly disturbed about what had happened.

On yet a different note, I have had an extremely worthwhile and uplifting experience outside the Waitrose supermarket Ruislip. This is a very busy store and I enjoy collecting there, as it is easy to park and the entrance where I stand is readily accessible and often surrounded by a lovely selection of potting plants and flowers.

On a few occasions I have met with Eric a well-known Big Issue vendor and we always had a good chat. He was full of interesting stories, especially about the magazine. I remember telling him that I had met the author of the book 'A Street Cat Named Bob', a biographical account of a homeless man and his cat Bob. I think the cat passed away in 2020. I told Eric that the author came to speak to a group of young people I was working with about being homeless and how the Big Issue had saved him, but primarily how his life had turned around due to the cat.

The story and film were very moving, yet Eric's story was far more complex. He had left Ireland, divorced, lost his job, suffered from ill-health and had become penniless, and he told me how hard it was being a Big Issue seller. He pretty much worked seven days a week, collecting at Waitrose over the weekend and standing around the Covent Garden area and in the city during the week. He mentioned that he was very fortunate in that he was often given a free breakfast by Pret a Manger in Covent Garden at around 5:30 in the morning, and this gave him a good chance of capturing businessmen and women going to work who would buy a magazine. He said that he needed to sell more than twenty five copies a day in order to make a profit.

What I noticed about Eric was his popularity with both customers and staff in the store, all of whom seemed to know him and appreciate what he was doing for the charity and to support himself in making a living. People offered him tea and coffee or a cold drink, many purchasing a cake or sandwich for him from the store.

I was concerned that my presence so close to Eric might result in his selling fewer copies of the Big Issue, and that I too would do less well with my tin, as people were familiar with Eric and might not want to give twice in such close proximity. This did not really seem to happen, Indeed, we both did quite well, and I think Eric appreciated my being there too.

He mentioned to me that some of his colleagues had taken to holding small electronic cash machines, rather than handle cash for their sales, but the costs were too prohibitive for him.

I have not seen Eric for several months due to the lockdown and the pandemic. He was not a particularly well man and I do hope that he's managed to continue to sustain himself and is safe. This was the only time that I regularly collected in the same area and at the same time as another charity, but it did seem to work.

On one occasion whilst we were standing outside the store, it was pouring with rain and rather cold. Eric, as he always did, was given a couple of free hot drinks. I decided to go in and buy a drink but there was nobody serving in the cafe area. Then I remembered that Waitrose offered a free cup of coffee with a receipt of purchase. I did not have such a receipt, so asked at customer service if I could purchase a cup of coffee from the free drink area as no-one was in the store café. Customer service said this would be fine, but I would need my own cup... Now I was really desperate for a hot drink.

Of course, I had not brought a cup with me, so despondently had to admit defeat and return to my collecting area and resume collecting.

Within 5 minutes a lovely member of staff presented me with a brand-new cup as a gift from the store, thanking me for being a charity collector and apologising for my struggle in getting a well-deserved cup of coffee. She told me to go into the store and help myself to one.

I really was speechless. This was such a wonderful gesture. I posted the story on Facebook and wanted to share it here. A random act of kindness can make such a difference.

Other such kind acts have been shown to me over the years, I remember collecting in the Edgware area over a Summer period and it being very hot. On two occasions someone unknown to me came up with a cold bottle of water saying , *"you must be thirsty", "thank you for doing this".*

Similar to this, the store manager of a very small Tesco Express, brought me a cup of coffee whilst collecting over the Winter holidays. This was very generous as it was the busiest time of the year for the store, I was probably unintentionally, in the way, yet the manager found the time to bring me over a steaming hot drink with a Kit Kat. She thanked me for volunteering for the charity.

On both occasions, it was very nice to feel appreciated and very rare to receive a free drink!

As I mentioned in Chapter 1, I had considerable experience working in the charity sector over several years, latterly, as a Director of a faith-based volunteering network, it is these random acts of kindness and the attitude of gratitude that have sustained me and I suggest so many others.

Tin Collecting is not just about the money. I remember collecting about 8 years ago in Sainsbury's in Stanmore. One Friday morning a small senior lady approached me and said she had just retired as a counsellor working with people with learning difficulties. She now had time on her hands and wanted to contribute using her skill set. She offered to volunteer as a tin collector for one day a week. Such an offer was not so unusual, but this lady has also continued to volunteer weekly as a mentor for individuals with special needs, offering learning support.

It is relatively rare to encounter a person with such a generosity of spirit.

Chapter 6: Starters for Ten!

Some of the Top Ten Best excuses for not putting any money in the tin

I have observed on an average collecting day probably a third of all those people out shopping drop some money in the tin, the others either look away, look through me and or offer an excuse for not donating.

I have listed here the best responses and excuses for not donating, some of them feasible, but often feeble.

Top Ten Excuses

1. **I gave earlier**

   This is the most popular/common excuse and I suggest that around half of those not donating will offer it.

   This excuse, is occasionally justifiable, especially if another collector had been in the same shop earlier, or in the proceeding few days, collecting for my charity, or even for a different good cause.

2. **Sorry love or Sorry, I have no cash on me**

   Two possibilities; either that person literally has no coins to put into the tin, or alternatively, they had no intention of giving.

   Either way, and although we are an increasingly cashless, card only society, I have always considered this to be a rather weak excuse. My retort to the comment is usually, *'I do take credit cards and all notes'.*

   Most people have at least some change on them, even if it is just a few coppers. What always makes me intensely angry is to later see those same shoppers returning their trolleys and redeeming their £1 coin. This leads nicely to the next excuse.

3. **I'm coming back. I'm just taking my shopping to the car and will give you the £1 once I have returned my trolley**

   Of course, most of these people, I never see again!

4. I contribute to your charity by standing order regulariy

and this goes together with ...

5. I never give to charities in this way

Sometimes this particular comment ends up in a rather abusive conversation regarding the national charity system, with people wanting to discuss charity giving in general. Asking me why the Government does not provide funds to charities. Not only would they want to discuss the percentages raised by collecting, but I would frequently be asked what proportion of the funds collected in the tin goes directly to the charity.

This of course is a fair question and I give the honest answer, which is over ninety five percent. However, I get very cross with the follow up question ...*'and how much do you personally receive for collecting?'*

Also irksome is the comment, *'there are too many of you charity people collecting in this way and it's very annoying'.....*

Yes, I have stock answers, but frequently have been left with the feeling that I was a scapegoat for people's misconceptions. Charity tin collecting and it is effectiveness is the reason why so many charities resort to this very simple and effective means of attracting donations from the public.

6. Sorry love I can't stop. I'm too busy. I'm just rushing in to pick up xy and/or z

A high percentage of those not giving use this excuse. I have often noticed that it is more likely to be used when collecting at an express store in a petrol station, and I do understand that here people are genuinely keen just to fill up their cars, pay for their petrol and get on their way.

7. **I do support other charities and I give to them- I just can't spread my money so thinly!**
   There's nothing to say to this one.

8. **I'll see you when I finish my shopping**
   This is a very frequently used excuse. Sometimes I remember them saying it and cheekily jog their memory as they exit. I say, *'Hi, remember me, I'm still here!'*

9. **Ignoring tactic**
   Probably, in the top two excuses is the ignoring tactic. Those people who say nothing but just pass by, eyes averted as if I was invisible. They carry on with a purposeful intent to do whatever they have to do. I do not like this at all. I would rather them say to me *'not today'*, or *'sorry, I've no change'*. Ignoring me, a volunteer collector, is in my opinion just downright rude and offensive.

10. **No excuse**
    In my book, there is no excuse for not giving anything. In the charity business, every penny counts'. This applies to the charity tin collector. If everyone puts a penny in the tin ... job done!

Top Ten Tips for would be collectors

Obviously, I do not have all of the answers for collecting money as a charity tin collector, but over the last decade I have noticed certain pointers which should definitely assist would be collectors, as well as a number of no-go areas.

Here are my Top Ten Tips: -

1. **Always check out the best footfall area**

   Before you start collecting, take a few moments, look around you to see which is the most popular entry point. Sometimes there are several entrances, and you should position yourself in the busiest one. Don't worry if you need to change to a different access point part way through your collecting period, as certain times of the day some exits and entrances are busier than at other times.

2. **Never sit down**

   I know sometimes it is impossible to stand for the whole two or three hours of the collecting period. But I have found that you need to be moving around and continually visible. So, unless you really need to sit down, position yourself, and if possible, keep moving in a very small area. This keeps you actively in the eye of those who potentially might put money in your tin. In my experience sitting down is low visibility, and **being visible is key to a successful collection**.

3. **Be in the space - be visible**

   Own the space! If you have to sit down or are unable to find a good standing position, ensure you are wearing a charity lanyard or something that creates high visibility for you as a collector. Perhaps, a funny hat or a bright scarf or the charity tee shirt. In my case, I tend to have about me not just the collecting tin, but also a large print notice about the charity that can be clearly seen and/or a clear hand-held sign. Where possible and if allowed, have a small table to display any charity literature. This should be in close proximity to where you are standing.

4. **Don't be a wall flower, be a sunflower**

   A bright smile, a catchy phrase, handing out stickers or free chocolates at certain times of the year especially Christmas or Easter Holidays is always a popular move. Some collectors over the Christmas break wear a Santa hat, and I always have a free chocolate to give out irrespective of whether money is put in my tin.

5. Make that tin work for you

Always put a few coins in the tin before you start your collecting experience. You do not have to shake it, but it does help to hear the money jangle. Hold the tin at chest level, do not hold it loosely down by your side. It must be seen and must also have a charity name or logo on it, clearly indicating who you are collecting for. After all, you are collecting for a charity, you should be proud of the charity and show it off, clearly holding your tin high!

6. Walk tall

You are only there for a couple of hours. You are an ambassador for the charity. Wear your charity badge with pride. Make sure you know about the charity. Why you are collecting, how it uses the money raised, and how you can help. People would often ask me, where does the money go? How much money do you need to raise? How much money is going to administration?

Make sure you know the answers to these questions. I have found that in answering with informed knowledge, people become interested and may want to donate more money than they had previously considered, they may even ask about volunteering for the charity!

They like to think that their donation goes directly to the work of the charity, so have the answers ready, Donors want to be donating towards something of value, so it is important that you can pinpoint specific items, areas of work or projects that your charity is supporting through the money you are raising.

7. Body language

Whilst I always prefer to stand, it is equally important to look happy. Eye contact is very important. Smile with your eyes as well with your mouth. Hopefully, you do enjoy the role BUT even if it is a rainy day and you are feeling a little down, it's important to look as if you are enjoying what you are doing.

So, always smile and say, *'good morning'* or *'good afternoon'*. We Brits like to comment on the weather, so pay attention to whether it is sunny or cold, and you can even apologise for the rain! Remember that if it is coming up to a seasonal holiday, to comment about the time of year. Be friendly, but not overly so - you do not want to drive shoppers away through your chatter. On a personal note, in the Northwest London area where I might be collecting on a Friday, prior to the Jewish Sabbath, I would offer a traditional greeting of *'Shabbat Shalom'*, which means peaceful Shabbat, and this usually goes down well and is rewarded with money being dropped into my tin. And importantly, do not look as if it is a chore for you to be collecting, remember that just by standing proud and smiling you can affect the mood of a potential donor. **You have a very limited time to catch the eye and or make an impact, use that time well**.

I also happen to like singing and whistling and for me this is a good way of drawing attention to myself and my tin collecting, so be creative about your presence.

During the 2012 London Olympics I collected wearing an Olympic T shirt and holding a ball and bucket. I would offer children an opportunity to try and throw the ball into the bucket. And I would say, *'Im collecting today whilst, hopping or running on the spot".* It certainly made people laugh and me stand out and be more visible!!

8. **Always remember that people go into a supermarket primarily to do their shopping**

   They do not want to be harangued by a tin collector. But a small gesture and a smile irrespective of whether a donation is in the tin, goes a long way to making someone feel good about the day ahead. Say thank you!

9. **Don't forget that you are there as a good will gesture from the supermarket**

   Never abuse that generosity, always say hello to the manager and staff before you start your collecting experience, and always remember to thank the manager when you leave.

10. **Have catch phrases to hand**

    Apart from *'Good morning'* and *'Good afternoon*, I might say *'any loose change, any coins in your coat or pennies in your pocket',* I like alliteration... But I often add jokingly, *'I take credit cards and notes'*.

For me, being able to retort in a friendly, cheeky way has worked. In Judaism, its known as Chutzpah... BUT do not use cheek if you are uncomfortable with it, it simply won`t be effective.

Finally, I noted a post here from a website about charity collecting and perhaps this sums it up:-

'I was in a Tesco yesterday, feeling ill, getting a little bit of shopping for my family and my four boys, and my mind was occupied (lots going on and racing to another kids party deadline). As I pushed the heavy trolley of groceries from the till, through the usually busy part between where you checkout and leave the building, some magnificent trolley manoeuvring is usually required. I spotted an old bloke at the side, holding a charity bucket unenthusiastically. As I passed, he muttered something about whatever charity it was. I passed with a quick, sorry, I'm a card only gal'.

Smile
Make eye contact
Be polite and friendly
Be willing and able to speak about your charity
Remember to say thank you for any donation, however small
Be in the space - Position yourself well
Hold a visible sign (The sign shown on the Fundraising detective site) - STOP, LOOK, GIVE! Every Penny counts is very clever and effective
Look presentable
Always wear your lanyard or charity T shirt
Remember: You only have a few seconds to make an impact!!!

Chapter 7: Legal Issues

Legislation for charity tin collecting and common mis-understandings

A common, but incorrect assumption is that you must stay silent and are not permitted to rattle or shake your tin. So, to clarify, and contrary to popular belief, shaking or rattling your tin is perfectly legal, though maybe a little annoying.

However, there are, for obvious reasons, strict rules regarding charity street collections. As we all know, restrictions can change, but these are the regulations current at the time of going to press.

The top ten rules

1. You must not begin collecting before 9:00am, Monday to Saturday, or 10:00am on Sundays and public holidays, or continue after 7:00am on any day (you can arrange and agree different charity time collecting within individual stores).
2. You must not position yourself within three metres of a shop entrance or a cash point machine.
3. Your location and any stand must not affect other businesses.
4. You must wear an ID badge that includes your identity as a fundraiser, specifies for whom you are raising money, and contains contact details for the relevant charitable institution or third-party organisation. Your ID badge must be clearly displayed and should not be tampered with. The badge must be fixed to the upper part of your body and should be at least the size of a credit card. It must be

signed or authorised in some way by the relevant agency or charity. Finally, it must be accessible for people with sight difficulties.

5. Your tin must be sealed and clearly labelled with the name of the Charity.

6. For more information check out admin@fundraisingregulator.org.uk.

Additional common courtesies to which I adhere to are: -

7. Always check in with the store manager before you begin collecting.

8. Whilst it is, in any event, important security-wise that the supermarket knows you are there, it is good for both you and the charity, to say hello and introduce yourself.

9. Check occasionally with the charity coordinator for whom you collect, that all permissions for you to be on site are in place.

10. Adhere to any specific requests from individual supermarkets shops.

Chapter 8: Valuing volunteers

Volunteers are often the lifeblood of a charity. They need to be properly inducted, valued, thanked and, of course, ready for the task in hand.

Charities do sometimes overlook their volunteers and fail to support them effectively. This leads to dissatisfaction, and ultimately to an absence of volunteers.

There is a new charity industry, volunteer management, with several books explaining how to best manage volunteers in order to dissipate such dissatisfaction, encourage retention and ensure that the charity and volunteer are in tune. In summary it comes down to these three Rs.

Recruit, Retain and Reward

Whilst I have not specifically mentioned volunteer recruitment, my introduction highlights how I was recruited, I was cajoled and persuaded. I was made to feel I had something to offer and that my contribution would be important and compliment my already busy schedule. The following tips are for charities to ensure that they prepare their volunteers for the best possible experience, ensuring that volunteers are recruited, retained, and rewarded.

Whilst focusing on charity tin collecting, these tips do have general applications, and should be standard good practice for all charities working with their volunteers.

One of my fellow Harrow Mencap volunteers is also a service user. She is great fun and is one of the most regular volunteers having been collecting for seven years, often up to three times per week.

This is what she told me, *"I enjoy collecting for Harrow Mencap as it is a worthwhile cause and I enjoy seeing and interacting with the public. I like collecting in two particular supermarkets, Tesco in Pinner and Stanmore Sainsburys. They always provide me with a chair to sit on which is very helpful to me. I would like a more noticeable sign too, as it can help me collect more money as I have to sit down.. Collecting allows me to get out of my flat and interact with people"*. She mentioned the funniest thing that happened to her recently, was when *"one mum gave her toddler some cash to put in the bucket, but he refused to let go of the money, so nothing was put in my tin!!!".* Thanks, Hannah, for all you do for Harrow Mencap and I do hope she gets her new sign soon!

Another service user has been collecting for ten years. He is fun, popular and everyone knows him...he says, *"I love collecting as I like talking to people".* He probably collects a couple of days a week. In a couple of stores, he is so well known, he is welcomed into the staff area so he can make himself a hot drink.

Top Ten Tips for Valuing Volunteers

1. Always ensure that any volunteer is given a proper induction into the role. This must include written information about the charity, any legislation, or rules that the individual needs to follow and details of the dos and don'ts of charity tin collecting.

2. It is always helpful for a volunteer collecting for the first time to have someone in a supportive role, a physical presence, standing close by. This is particularly relevant for a charity where its clients/users may also be collectors, (such as Harrow Mencap, where our service users love to be out collecting and contributing to their charity), it can make them feel less nervous and more comfortable in their new role. Also ensure you notify the store management, so they are aware of any special needs.

3. Volunteers should be provided with the resources required to do their job effectively. In collecting, this is obviously a tin or bucket.... but should also include an identifiable up to date personal charity ID card (a lanyard is best) and any fliers, materials, or giveaway stickers. Charities are in competing markets, especially in raising money through tin collecting, it is therefore important that they stand out or have a USP (unique selling proposition), where possible.

4. Good charities will also provide basic necessities for their helpers.

   For example, in hot weather volunteers, who may be standing for a long period of time in the heat, should be given a bottle of water, or at least encouraged to take one with them.

5. The charity should send regular communications to volunteers. Not bombarding them, but it is important that volunteers are informed of events, programmes, and any changes within the charity. Furthermore, collectors do like to know how much is raised and how the money is used.

6. It is generally accepted, that where volunteers perform similar roles, they become specific identifiable groups. Charities should arrange for volunteers to meet occasionally, and for them to get to know one another. This should initially occur when new individuals are recruited, in order that together they receive a briefing, hear about the role and are made to feel part of a team.

7. Although a charity collector might not need training per se, a good charity will provide: -

   - A basic induction session providing information an introduction to the charity and about the role of the volunteer

   - A session about the charity tin collector, volunteering in supermarkets, what the volunteer can/cannot do

- A few tips on collecting.....this book would be a good resource to use!!!

8. Charity tin collection can occasionally be stressful. I have shown in a previous chapter, how occasionally, people will approach and want to share their story with you, and you have to listen. Not all stories are pleasant. Additionally, as I have also mentioned, some people can be downright rude and offensive, and this can be upsetting.

   To that end, volunteers need to know there is provision to offload and share. Good charities will have a support system in place.

9. Well run charities have groups or committees made up of service users, clients and volunteers, who have direct access to key staff. They can meet as and when, but woe betide the charity that does not allow for these voices to be heard!

10. Whilst charities are generally financially challenged and members and volunteers do not like to see hard earned cash wasted, a good charity will reward its volunteers in a small way. A thank you card, or letter a couple of times a year, sent with the charity`s newsletter, a shopping or coffee voucher from one of the supermarkets, (no more than the cost of a coffee and a cake), are very good ways of thanking volunteers for the numerous hours they give.

Chapter 8: Valuing volunteers

Chapter 9: Covid-19 and Collecting, plus, of course...Top 10 Tips!

Most of this book has been written during the Covid-19 pandemic, a defining period of time, and as I write this chapter, we are in a second wave and a further lockdown. It is early November 2020, lockdown restricts movement which means we can only venture out for necessities, and exercise. Places of worship are closed again, as are restaurants and other non-essential retail outlets, as well as most of the hospitality sector. These are all precautionary measures. Charity collecting has again come to a halt.

In this challenging time, the charity sector has been decimated, as much needed funds have not been forthcoming. After months in lockdown, cancelled events and limited fundraising activity, non-profit organisations across the UK and Europe are facing massive funding shortfalls. Many charities have now laid staff off. For Harrow Mencap, so reliant on volunteer charity collectors, this year has been devastating.

There is a desperate need to get back out there and start fundraising, but the priority, of course, has to be ensuring that fundraisers are doing this in a way that is safe, respectful and abides with social distancing recommendations.

Cash is known to collect and host a range of bacteria; **E.Coli**, **MRSA** and **Listeria** are just a few that have been identified on notes and coins. Despite cash's dirty reputation, the risk that cash poses with regard to spreading coronavirus is not clearly established. As I write, no studies have yet been undertaken hat conclusively demonstrate that ability of notes and coins to spread COVID-19.

At the time of writing, there is no data looking at physical money in particular – all we know is that transmission occurs most commonly through droplets of saliva containing the infection. If these can survive on money for long enough (which the evidence suggest it probably can), and if those using cash proceed to touch their eyes, noses or mouths after handling it, then it's reasonable to assume that the use of cash can indeed to some extent contribute to the spread of COVID-19. It is for this reason that the **World Health Organisation** have advised the public to wash their hands after dealing with cash, especially if they are holding, or eating food at the same time.

Friday, August 14th 2020 – the date of my first post-lockdown outing to collect for Harrow Mencap. This was the second week the charity had organised collections during the pandemic and much discussion had taken place, and information disseminated regarding how to collect, including changes in procedure, in particular, the special steps required for collecting during these extraordinary times.

We were very fortunate in that one or two supermarkets had agreed for us to begin our charity tin collecting but were quite rightly expressing concerns as to how it would be organised. What was important and agreed was the need to avoid any physical contact and of course to wear a mask.

As we had to maintain social distancing with the general public, we were provided with a charity bucket to ensure that people did not get too close to us, and to facilitate dropping the money into the tin without touching it, or the need to be near the collector, as would have been the case previously.

Volunteers like myself were given a sheet explaining how our charity had been supporting its clients during the last few months, and, also informing people of a new option, the ability to donate through texting.

The stint for collecting was still two hours and we were advised, due to the incredibly hot preceding few days, to bring a water bottle and possibly wear a hat. We were also asked to collect only outside the store, and to wear a mask at all times.

For my first supermarket collection I noticed that they had introduced a one way in and one way out system. I needed to be visible and place my bucket strategically, so as not to get in the way. This was challenging. I was fortunate that the weather had changed, and it was rather overcast and a much cooler day. Notwithstanding this, wearing a mask for two hours and trying to smile and maintain eye contact was difficult!

I was despairing at the outset, as people were saying they had no cash, they could not stop and of course most people didn't want to hang around in the supermarket for any longer than necessary. I also recognised that the speed in decline of cash use over the last couple of years had accelerated during the pandemic and many more people were now using cards, or paying via their phone, no longer carrying any coins or notes.

Dispiritingly, collecting was very slow. Of course, I recognised one or two people, and a few recognised me, so that slowly coins were put in the tin. A few shoppers chatted to me, but I was beginning to be concerned as to whether the exercise was going to prove worthwhile and whether fundraising through tin collecting would ever be the same again . My colleague had informed me that it had been the same the previous week, and I was realising that the impact of collecting money during a pandemic, wearing a mask, combined with lack of cash and people's limited financial circumstances could result in our collections being vastly reduced. I was considering that maybe at the end of the first hour I would call my colleague to say that the collecting was not working out. Then, as luck would have it, a wonderful woman from a church in neighbouring Northwood approached me. Anne said, *"how sad it was that the local Mencap group could no longer use the church for their coffee and chat mornings, due to the pandemic"*, and she praised the good work of Harrow Mencap.

I saw her go to her wallet and knew that she would put in a coin or two. However, she took out a £10 note and put it in the bucket. This really made my day, and I was no longer despondent. Little did she know it, but due to her act of kindness, I made my mind up and stayed for my last hour.

Unbelievably, two further people each gave me a 10-pound note. In nearly ten years of collecting, I had never before been given more than one £10 pound note at any time!

I observed several things from that experience.

Top Ten Observations Learned

1. There are still many generous people who care about others.
2. Charity collecting at a time of financial depression is extrermely challenging.
3. People will not make time to text donations, they either give you money there and then, or collectors must use a portable card machine.
4. Wearing a mask inhibits visual contact and facial expression, although one can see eyes, you cannot really see a smile or other facial reactions.
5. As the shopping experience has changed, and shoppers rush to complete their buying. It is important for the collector to make themselves clearly visible and to articulate very briefly and eruditely why financial support is so important for a charity at this particular time.
6. There is greater need for larger visual information. Time is of the essence and a picture tells a thousand stories.
7. A bucket is less tactile than a hand held charity tin, and more likely to be ignored. I placed the bucket on a separate seat in order to elevate it.
8. The layout of the store will have changed to comply with social distancing, which affects both the position of the collector and familiarity of the supermarket with the shopper.
9. Fewer people are out shopping. It is uncertain if the high street and retailers will ever recover from this pandemic in the same form as before. Footfall in most stores is declining as more people, particularly senior citizens and others shielding, turn to online shopping.

10. We need to consider what a new normal will look like for charity tin collecting in supermarkets. Whilst supermarkets are holding their own, how charities are welcomed and engaged with them in the future will need to be monitored.

Chapter 10: The final word

If you have reached this concluding chapter, thank you.

I encourage you to read the Appendices, especially Ken Burnett's piece on his charity tin collecting experience for charity.

2020 has been a very difficult year across the world and 2021 seems to be following suit. So many of us have been personally affected by Covid-19, and its knock-on effects have been and, as I write, continue to be, horrendous.

In the preceding chapter, I share my Covid-19 collecting experiences. Here, I ask whether charity collecting will ever return to its pre-Covid-19 ways.

It bears repeating, this type of fundraising with people putting loose change into a tin or bucket, is ever more challenged. People carry less change, we are an increasing cashless society, there is less disposable income than a year or two ago, and it appears that fewer volunteers are available. And then there is the COVID-19 factor.

Whilst at the time of writing, there are no studies explicitly linking the use of cash to the transmission of COVID-19, research suggests that note and coins could play a part in spreading this disease.

Contactless transactions are on the rise. According to figures from GoodBox, there were **720 million contactless card transactions in January 2020** (before lockdown measures were bought in), which represents a 12.3% increase from the same time last year. This trend is only expected to continue, especially given that the maximum limit for individual contactless transactions has been increased from £30 to £45.

The decreasing use of cash is an issue for charities looking to raise funds during these difficult times and in the future. Charity tin collections are a critical component of donation sources for many of them.

Ultimately, charities must recognise the need to change their fund-raising programmes and in particular the reliance on tin collecting. They must be willing and able to adapt, as I fear if they do not, their future may be bleak.

Yet, despite an uncertain economic outlook, the public's willingness to donate seems not to have waned – the monumental achievement of Captain Tom Moore, raising more than £30 million for the NHS, is testament to this.

Clearly, looking forward, charities will need to alter the ways in which they collect donations, perhaps moving away from volunteer-manned cash collections, and embracing a better use of technology. Donations made through websites assume more importance, as social distancing is likely to continue in some form for a long time yet.

Charities will need to be increasingly creative in attracting donations.

Since its inception in 2016, GoodBox has supported the charity sector during challenging times, be it an ever-growing cashless society or the effects of a global pandemic.

How? GoodBox provides charities with a single point of entry to a range of digital fundraising tools and technology.

'We're proud to have partnered with over 1,500 charities across the UK, including the Church of England, Christian Aid and Natural History Museum. Most importantly, we've helped charities increase their donation income by up to 85% as donors reach for their cards and phones to show support.

Coronavirus has accelerated the move towards a cashless society and will transform the global fundraising landscape.

During this time, GoodBox is working harder than ever to provide effective and intuitive innovation to the sector'.

Information from Joe Geary, Marketing Manager of GoodBox,

(Contactless Charity Donation Boxes), www.goodbox.com.

In the interim a donation of £1 will be made to Harrow Mencap for every copy of this book that is sold by myself or the publisher, Russell House Publishing Ltd.

Appendix 1: Supermarkets with tin rating as collecting venues

I have rattled my tin in the following supermarkets each is given an equivalent of a TripAdvisor style Tin Rating which will be explained in the appendices at the end of the booklet. Although the supermarkets mentioned here are local to my area, the ratings reflect those pertinent and applicable aspects of what contributes to a good supermarket collecting experience.

Thanks to the following supermarkets:-

Tesco Pinner green

Tesco Express Canons Corner

Tesco Harrow, (large supermarket)

Sainsbury's Pinner

Sainsbury's Edgware Broad walk

M&S food store Pinner

M&S Ruislip High Street

ALDI Kingsbury

ASDA South Harrow

Waitrose Ruislip

Morrison's Hatch End

Morrison's Harrow

Iceland Harrow

There are a couple here with no star rating. This is because they made limited impact, and I can truthfully say that while I know that I was asked to collect there, I am unable to recollect the venue. This is not necessarily a bad result, as they were not high scoring, neither were they low.

Key to Ratings

 - One tin indicated a very ordinary experience. Whilst the shop is on the main high Street in the centre of Harrow it's footfall on the couple of days when I was collecting was not very productive and therefore it didn't rate. Furthermore, it was difficult to park near the store. I remember standing outside in the front of the shop pretty much at a loose end. I even recollect texting our collecting tin coordinator and suggesting we refrain from collecting at this particular store as it was so quiet. No doubt this would not be the case for other stores in the same chain, and in any event, the footfall may have improved.

 - A few stores received a two-star rating. In the case of the Asda and the Harrow Morrison's, the rating was given because both very large stores had entrances whereby access to the store was via a travellator. This meant as a collector I did not know whether to stand at the bottom of the travellator which was (for most people the exit out of the store), or to position myself at the top, the open entry into the store, catching people on the way in and or out.

One or two colleagues, I noted, would sit at the top, but I observed their trade was not too good as frequently the positioning was close to a seasonal offering and I think was in the way of the customers.

Regarding the Morrison's store another factor was the location of the signing in book, which alerts security and shop managers as to who is in the store at any one time. This was quite some distance from a collecting position. If no staff were manning that area, you wasted time waiting to sign yourself in. Signing in, is common and good practise.

Aldi in Kingsbury received two-star rating too, as the standing position is really between the exit and entrance, very close to the trolley and shopping basket area. For me it meant that several times in the given collecting time I was causing an obstruction! Additionally, the store had a couple of officious security guards who were doing a great job with suspicious customers, but it seemed as if I was also given the challenging look!

 - The vast majority of supermarkets came into the three-star rating bracket. This is because in my opinion, the position for a tin collector was fairly good and the overall experience was pleasant and sometimes memorable. All the stores in this group had available parking.

Whilst I have just said parking was available, Sainsburys in Stanmore has a 90-minute allowance. The first time I collected here, I didn't realise that on signing in I needed to notify the store that I was a charity collector and would be doing a two hour stint! Needless to say, I received a parking ticket, I wouldn't of course ask the charity to cover this, but did alert them to this issue. I contacted the company who owned the car park and explained my predicament. I was thankfully given a reprieve and now ensure I inform the desk when I am collecting there.

 - The recipients of this rating were awarded this due to the ease of parking, and or free parking, friendly staff and awareness of serviceuser's needs: i.e. providing a chair and simple signing process.

 - A five star award is all of the above, but where the staff welcome the volunteer collectors, offering hot or cold drinks etc.

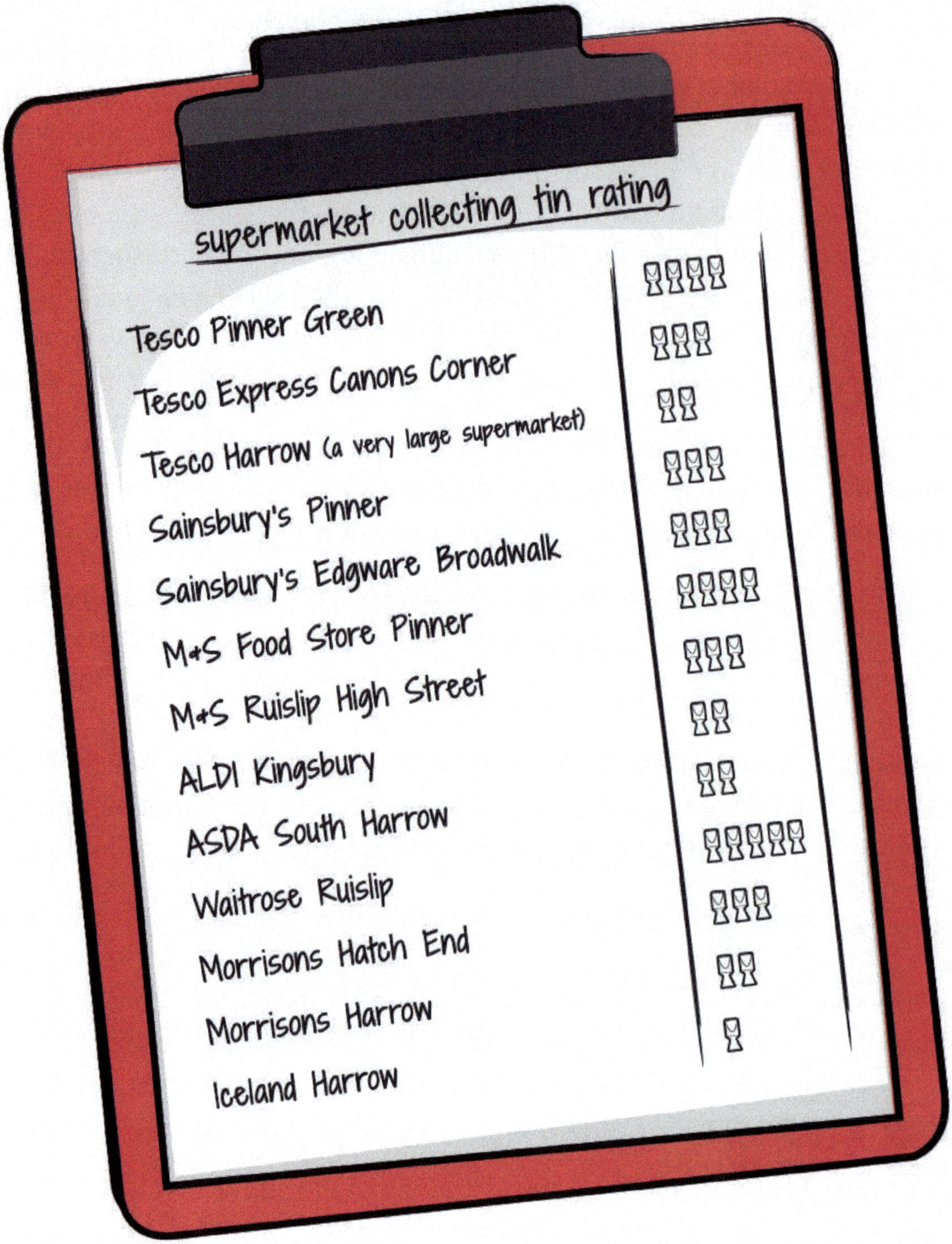
supermarket collecting tin rating
Tesco Pinner Green
Tesco Express Canons Corner
Tesco Harrow (a very large supermarket)
Sainsbury's Pinner
Sainsbury's Edgware Broadwalk
M+S Food Store Pinner
M+S Ruislip High Street
ALDI Kingsbury
ASDA South Harrow
Waitrose Ruislip
Morrisons Hatch End
Morrisons Harrow
Iceland Harrow

Appendix 2: A story that warmed the cockles of my heart

Thanks to Ken Burnett, its author, it appears here in full.

Ken is an international fundraising, marketing and communication specialist. www.kenburnett.com.

The collection: it is never too late to do something wonderful.

Spend a few hours collecting cash in a moderately busy concourse and you will learn a lot about people, their good bits and the bad.

It was cold and my feet hurt. I'd just been rejected, for the umpteenth time and been politely told off by a station guard for rattling my bucket. '*It annoys the staff*,' he explained. '*Well, if you do it too much it does*.'

Then a dignified middle-aged man with a beard, trailing his family behind him, stepped from the throng that was flowing from the shoppingcentre and stopped, right in front of me. He looked me full in the eye as he dug inside his voluminous winter coat, pulled out his pocketbook and proceeded to empty its contents into my bucket. My spirits soared. Thenhe gathered his family around him, mother, teenage son and two younger daughters and spoke to them for a while in a language I could not catch. Soon they were all rummaging among their clothing. The procedure tooksome time. Then the teenage son, beaming from ear to ear, came over topour handfuls more cash into my bucket.

'*Thank you*,' he said, then bounced off with a spring in his step to catch his departing family. For the first time that day, I felt great.

I was with my wife, Marie, and younger son, Charlie, standing at the top of the escalators in Bond Street station, just outside the barriers. It was Easter Sunday and, though a lot thinner than we had anticipated, a constant flow of shoppers was coming through. Marie and I each had a bucket, Charlie had two and we had a three-hour stint to complete. We were collecting money for Syria's refugees and those displaced by civil war inside the country, three million-plus and growing by the day.

That sea of faces rising from the escalators is daunting, first time you confront it. They come in surges and are a mixed amorphous mass. The last thing they are expecting to greet them is three white Brits in a line, rattling buckets. Not all are pleased. Most are indifferent. Some are, well, extraordinary. If only we could have an announcement at the foot of the escalator, saying, *'get your money ready!'*

Bond Street station is the world in microcosm, a mini United Nations. In our three hours it seemed as if every conceivable ethnic grouping filed past us. We could not help but notice which were the more generous. It was not the white British middle classes, far from it. Charlie felt South Asians gave most to him – a Japanese woman with a huge smile gave him half the contents of her purse. A Chinese woman with a cheeky grin slipped me a tenner. But it was middle-eastern people, mainly Muslims, who put most in my bucket. Marie's too.

Young couples are the least generous, or so it seemed to us, with older couples not far behind. Some people love givers and giving, so support us with looks. Others prefer to look away.

Three people come at me from different angles all at the same time. Briefly the bucket gets busy. I do not know who to thank first, so I thank the whole foyer, loudly. The station manager beams. Everyone is looking at me now.

Then there is a lull. Busyness comes and goes, but the shoppers are few and I fear it is not enough. We are doing badly. Someone tells us that most shops are closed. For a full 20 minutes everyone ignores us. Then Marie says, *'I've got three tenners'*. I think of Pavarotti and Co, but resist breaking into song.

Smile, make eye contact. The brightest eyes are the most generous, there is no doubting that. The bucket feels heavier but is not really. We stand stock still, not rattling, not moving, buckets aloft. Then in unison, we give them a sway.

Children really enjoy giving. A man stood in front of me for several minutes digging into his pockets. Then, having found his oyster card, he left without giving. Behind him a gaggle of Syrian women, hands ornate with henna designs, ask if they can take a photo, then give me a pile of cash. *'Here's £10.00'*, says another woman. *'Have a nice day and thank you very much for what you're doing'*. Smarter-dressed people are not more generous. Expensive coats do not give, we reckon.

A Turkish boy, maybe eight or nine, asks me what I am doing. *'Why are they fighting*?' he asks. *'What's a refugee?'* I try to explain but cannot give him a decent justification. *'It's just bad'*, I say. *'People have to leave their homes and loved ones in the middle of the night'*.

He looks about to get emotional. *'I'll speak to my auntie'*, he promises, *'and come back'*. He did not, though he tried, I am sure. And used some of my lines too, I bet. Perhaps, as he grows, he will think about it...

A young Italian man asks me the way to Buckingham Palace. I oblige, though he gives me nothing but a smile. Then another chap asks me why I am doing this. I should have quoted some lines from A. A. Gill in today's Sunday Times, but I did not bring it with me.

'As I watch, figures appear out of the darkness, bent double under sacks. Families hold hands, moving past us like heavy ghosts. This is the last leg of one of the most dangerous journeys on Earth'.

Gill goes on, in similar, graphic vein. Note for next collection: bring a supply of moving emotional stories, because sometimes people want to talk. '*Why isn't there more on the News?*' one man asks. Marie responds accurately. '*I don't know*'.

Just as we were getting ready to go, a woman in a headscarf walked upto Charlie and asked what he was doing. She was young, about 25, and crying, big tears running down her cheeks. As she left him to visit the cashmachine in the corner of the concourse, her eyes met mine. Minutes latershe was back, clutching money. She did not want to speak, just put two notes into my bucket, urgently. I watched till, with a gentle push from her,they were gone. Then so was she. I was overcome.

Our time was up. We thanked London Transport's wonderful people, signed out then headed off to find a pub, thirsty and a bit tearful. As we sauntered down Brook Street, a passing gent hailed Charlie. '*For Syria*', he said, putting a fiver in Charlie's bucket. For a minute I thought Charlie was going to say, '*But we've finished for the day*'. He did not.

'*You're a toff,*' he said, beaming.

Truly it is never too late, to do something wonderful.

At one point, just after setting off, I had wondered to myself whether I shouldn't just put a bunch of notes in the bucket and go home. I'm so glad now that I didn't.

Appendix 3: Ten is the magic number

The subtitle of this book is, Tens of Tips for Charity Tin Collecting, which refers to the numerous references I have made throughout to the number ten in the form of Top Ten Tips. Indeed, there is a chapter entitled Starter for Ten!!

This is because I find it easier to remember in short sharp summarised point form and realised that a list of top tens, such as, suggestions, songs, books etc, is certainly more digestible and memorable. On researching more about why ten might have a significant role to play in list forming, (listicles – a new word I have come across), I discovered this piece on the internet, which I have adapted slightly.

With thanks to POYNTER – the Poynter Institute for media studies Florida USA.

I have used several Top Ten tips throughout this guide. I find them to be easy on the eye and more memorable, offering user friendly summaries and information. I am not alone in doing this and have provided this appendix to indicate the significance of the number ten.

There is a great deal of historical significance behind the number ten. There are Ten Amendments in the Bill of Rights and Ten Commandments. Number 10 is the home of the Prime Minister. And the metric system is a standard set of prefixes in powers of 10.

By now, Top Ten is a convention, but its origins may be in body parts: fingers and toes, hands, feet, digits and inches, so says journalist Rex Sorgatz [i] and media psychologist, senior editor of the Journal of Media Psychology, Stuart Fischoff [i], in an online article from Poynter.org.

The article notes that Rex Sorgatz[(i)], **has been creating lists of lists** since 2001, says *"lists have become increasingly common —They're catchy and easy to create, so it's not surprising that news sites publish them"*. But why are they so popular among would be writers like yours truly?

Here's the Top 10 reasons for creating Top 10's, summarised

1. They make us smarter – A written summary can be a quick way to facilitate learning.
   'lists can provide a thumbnail rundown of what or who is up and down, in and out, winning or losing'.

2. They are memorable.
   Lists make it easier to remember information because they break it up into parts. *'Psychology shows there is a certain amount of information people can juggle',* said Fischoff [(i)], *'if we can break things up into chunks of meaningful data, it's much easier for us to store and remember them'.* Sargatz [(i)] notes that attaching a number to information also helps. Numerous TV programmes offer the Top Ten funniest TV soap moments, or the Top 10 best adverts etc.

   People are more likely to remember the **Top Ten albums of the year**, for instance, if they see them laid out in a numbered list.

3. They are nostalgic and futuristic.
   Lists provide helpful summaries of what has happened throughout the year and can give us a reason to look ahead.

4. They explain and order our experiences.
   Some lists help answer the fundamental questions *'WHY?'*

   Why some healthy people contracted COVID-19.

   Why the most qualified candidate for a position will not always get the job.

5. Lists help us make sense of the world, and this clarity can prompt us to take action. Some lists naturally lend themselves to fun and interesting discussions. We can look at a list of the best books and talk about them with out literary group. Or we can share a list of Top 10 YouTube videos with friends.

6. They rank our views.
The way we react to lists says something about our personality. *'When we read a list of Top 10 movies, do we passively accept that these were the year's best movies, or do we feel the urge to refute what we see'.*

7. They express opinions.
No two lists are alike. If you look at five different lists of the Top 10 books of the year, they are likely to be divergent because they reflect differing opinions. Lists, Rex Sorgatz [(i)] said, *'give journalists a way to be super opinionated without seeming like it'.*

8. They capture cultures.
Rex Sorgatz [(i)] notes that, in the introduction to a list of the 100 best TV shows of all time, TV Critic James Poniewozik wrote: *'Lists are incredibly important. They are how we define what matters to us, what we want entertainment and art to do, what we expect of our culture'.* (Time Magazine, 5th September 2007).

Lists vary from culture to culture and looking at them can help us understand differences between societies. *'If you want to know a culture, and know what it values'*, Stuart Fischoff [(i)] said, *"Know what's in the top 10 lists".*

(i) Rex Sorgatz and Stuart Fischoff - pointer.org 16th November 2011.

9. They are practical.
Many of the How To's, published in the media are in the form of easy to read lists. Poynter.org publish such lists.

10 tips for moderating a successful live chat.

10 ways journalists can use Twitter before, during and after reporting a story.

10 tools that can help data journalist do better work, be more efficient.

10. They are motivational.
At the end or beginning of the year, people may have more time to do things they neglect throughout the year.

These are times when we make resolutions. *'Lists coincide with the end of the year and the holidays'.* Sorgatz said, *"because they're moments in time when we're travelling or trapped in out parents' house and we have more open time than we do the rest of the year".* Ref: Covid 19.

Appendix 4: Research

Gift Aid research commissioned by HMRC, (HM Revenue and Customs) in September 2016, estimated that money donations to collecting tins or buckets to be worth as much as £620m a year to the charity sector. The research also estimated that as much as 78 per cent of the population had made such a donation at least once in the previous 12 months. This research however did not stipulate what it meant by '*money to collecting tins or buckets*' and whether or not it included paper money donations.

A 2018 survey determined that children, young people and animal welfare jointly lead the list of the causes people say they donate to, with 26% of people saying they gave to each of those causes in the previous month. Peak months for giving money are November and December. This has become a yearly pattern largely due to established fundraising campaigns over this period. They are also the main months for cash donations.

Susan Pinkney, head of research at CAF, (Charities Aid Foundation), said that while coins remain an important donation channel for charities, the sector still needs support in handling the transfer to cashless donations from the government. *"It's brilliant that people donate millions of pounds a year in loose change – money put into collection tins or spent at charity stalls across the length and breadth of the UK"*.

"Cash is still by far the most common way people donate to charity, and nothing is easier than putting your hand in your pocket and putting a few coins into a collection. But we know that overall, cash transactions are falling. So, if cash becomes less and less popular in the future it's vital that

the government works with charities and the payment industry, to make sure giving remains as easy as tapping a card or putting a few coins in a tin".

See more at:

https://www.civilsociety.co.uk/news/donations-of-loose-change-worth-320m-a-year-for-charity-says-caf

Appendix 5: Some helpful online sites for collecting:

There are numerous charities offering advice on raising funds and charity tin collecting.

These words by the Marie Curie Charity sum up why charity tin collecting is worth while.....

'Whether it's your first time collecting for Marie Curie or you are a seasoned volunteer, your time and support really does make a difference. Not only is collecting hugely rewarding, it's also a great way to meet people and get involved in your local community'.

'One of the nice things about collecting is talking to people and hearing their stories. Often members of the public will talk about their loved ones and personal connections to Marie Curie when they see a collector, which can be a great reminder of the impact the money you collect could make'.

Checkout the following Top Ten online sites:-

1. https://www.fundraisingdetective.com
   Helping you solve your fundraising problems.

2, Prostatecanceruk.org
   The complete guide to fundraising collection boxes.

3. https://fundraisingexpert.com/collection-boxes

4. The British Lung Foundation. bfl.org.uk

5. https://www.charitychoice.co.uk/the-fundraiser/fundraising-type/street-fundraising
Practical advice and insight for the charity sector.

6. https://mariecurie.org.uk/get-involved/collecting
Top tips for collectors.

7. https://www.youtube.com/watch?v=CLex7JcwBRE
ICS Fundraising – Bucket Collections and /The Power of Difference

These are an easy to follow videos about bucket collecting do's and don'ts.

8. https://www.meresearch.org.uk/support-us/supermarket-collecting

9. https://www.ho-plastics.co.uk/blog/choosing-and-using-charity-collection-buckets, November 2014.
They manufacture charity collecting tins and buckets, and offer some very good advice for this type of fundraising.

10. https://www.rspca.org.uk/webContent/staticImages/fundraising/SupermarketColections.pdf

11. Harrowmencap.org.uk

Please note: At the time of going to print the above website details were correct. Online posts may become outdated with regards to rules on charity collecting, always check the most recent government legislation.